REGRESSIVE POETICS

ANNA McKERROW

KFS

NEWTON-LE-WILLOWS

Published in the United Kingdom in 2014
by The Knives Forks And Spoons Press,
122 Birley Street,
Newton-le-Willows,
Merseyside,
WA12 9UN.

ISBN 978-1-909443-34-1

The cover image is by Dylan Harris. Please visit his website at http://dylanharris.org/
to see more of his excellent work.

Supported using public funding by
LOTTERY FUNDED
ARTS COUNCIL ENGLAND

Table of Contents

Regressive Poetics   v

Until the Dreams Began Picking the Recurrence of the Streams   11

Omm Sety   20

Eyes Returning Red   24

The Truth Appeals to a Loss of Terms   27

The Protected Server is a Group of Action   30

Stereo References   34

Winifred   39

Foreign Highways   44

Where They Don't Penalise Tone Critique   49

Regressive Poetics

I became aware of the concept of reincarnation at a young age, being presented with the idea that our souls use the earth as a vast schoolroom, returning to it to learn new lessons over many lives, as a completely logical concept by my mother. I continue to view it as entirely likely.

When I was older I discovered that my grandmother had for many years been secretary and editor to A J Stewart, author of *Falcon: The Autobiography of His Grace James IV, King of Scots*. Ms Stewart's fascinating book was the account of her past life as James IV, and she was completely convinced of the veracity of her story.

The guiding ethos of this work is my interest in the correlations between artistic and spiritual practices, and the strong place of language within practices such as meditation, magic, divination etc. After producing a process-based poetic work on the tarot I wondered whether past life recall stories would be an interesting medium for a similar processual approach.

I am interested in the way that a past life "memory", or story, is accessed via a hypnotic state, and relayed to the hypnotist or therapist in a state very much like a waking dream. We have all had the experience of language in dreams, where the words that seem so profound in the dream are nonsense when awake.

There is also an element of translation or decryption present in past life tales, in the sense that they are usually relayed back in a somewhat fragmentary way from the border of the unconscious. In mediumship this is a common problem, because communicating with the spirit world is described as talking with someone very far away, or operating on a very different frequency of sound. Discrepancies occur.

I see now how we can wander and get lost in the memories of the automatist when we so-called dead try to communicate. This kind of mutual selection is bound to be what my friend Gerald calls a "mixed grill"

– Received from Winifred Coombe Tennant by Geraldine Cummins in *Swan on a Black Sea: A Study in Automatic Writing* eds Signe Toksvig, 1971.

I wanted to push this derangement of language another step further, this "mixed grill" of language from one side, death, being translated through to the other side, life.

I worked with a digital dictation app into which I read published accounts of past lives from a variety of sources. This produced its own version of the text, complete with interesting inaccuracies and juxtapositions and a surprising amount of digital and online-speak, which can only reflect the programming of the app to be sensitive to current technological jargon. In the way that the app "made sense" of what I gave it, we too tend to interpret accounts such as past life "memories" through the veils of historical fact, bias, scientific rationale, physics theory or personal prejudice.

With past life regression hypnotic work there is also the possible issue of suggestion on the part of the hypnotist/therapist, again echoing the possible adjustment of the text. This mediation is also common in mediumship, as mentioned above. In *Swan on a Black Sea*, the spirit of the very politically liberal Mrs Coombe-Tennant sometimes "transmitted" far more conservative political opinions, which was deemed to be the bias of the medium Miss Cummins' own beliefs on the original message.

Each poem in this collection is based on one particular past life story and is the result of translation and rewriting from the original text (the original experience) to a doubly mediated text – a version of the original mediated first by technology and second by the writer (me). Some pieces were recorded by the app direct from online videos rather than being read aloud by me. The poems are therefore subject to technological, programmed language bias and personal bias/artistic style on my part. This is an integral part of their being.

I found that this method gave me some linguistically interesting pieces which still managed to keep a sense of dreamlike mystery as well as highlighting the strange hyperreality of "remembering" a past life in such apparent detail. In these poems, the stories are trying to "get through", but there is an imperfect medium (me) using a flawed machinery.

– Anna McKerrow, April 2013

REGRESSIVE POETICS

Until the Dreams Began Picking the Recurrence of the Streams

click here to request the inter body/performance is when the secret details are only electric/not limited to stain the body/intended from the body/follow those ranges across distance -

I wished they'd hear that you could only follow those of your life/you need a special connection/he should know before a short distance -

I've chosen to use a digital Celtic or Britain/first to read the pain going far/sex you could know when you know the hate to touch up/it came actually between/the started to remember –

I closed my eyes and killed tests.

I realised that this was the award/retraining understanding/against the old women in a room/it was dawn/smell of smoke filled my past rocks/somehow powerful taste of pollution/lest I heard footsteps/and my preteen crew/stale footsteps came closer than ever passing right away/I swear a lot unkempt alone/another man of similar size on the floor was not really page-

bending me/I jumped into the moment/bending down anyone/quick new stuff/he threw me off, yelling in some strange directors/he felt the floor I crashed against/the wall for breast knocked out of me and/casting/I watched as the buyer looking them last act/like with a nice ethernet-

like portrait reading/suddenly his body working with death/I looked down at him/discussed content quickly/and the voice-

over woman calling on a farm/*what type of name is that* said like to open my eyes/close my eyes and labour and try to laugh myself/having a great imagination and steadily/I could not stop saying that I was going to bless a cleaner list of all/one who really got, been real, touched by another person/thank you for oil -

gas exploration/I wanted to be the procedure/I began working with a well-respected timekeeper/with her I was able to hear my insomnia/I can't understand how it happened/like tiny island hopping/affecting my present life/I would stay awake all night/and deterrent is dead/inside this ritual/burning in a past life online/I slept for late homes for the first time and

I'm living in America in the middle of the night/accelerating dream theatre.

I was an ancient fortification made a word/I close from a very different feeling like fabric/the lighthouse faint country-pronged spots filled with oil/hung from ceiling beans on Strickland pedestals/I live through the same scene of myself using a tiger to kill a beautiful woman on the back -

I continued on a woman dressed contract coloured clothes/I continued on the phone myself/interacting with various people after I'm here.

It was just a coincidence bathroom/clinically I had heard of lifting the course/war and the women wore beautiful clothes and jewellery/I was trying very hard to begin a path medication piece/when I was in the parties I felt egotistical/angry and completely self-absorbed after the question/I found it very distasteful to think I could have one tiny penis/she was so decided to forget about her and focus on my music limitation hygienist/wicked dreams of myself stuck in watching women being beheaded in front of me/until the dreams began picking the recurrence of the streams -

Then I found myself standing in the rain/again in an older fault/apparently excited to play with my hair/my clients/I looked nice in wonderfully creaming gold/a surge of love slept through me/possibly watched through my arms/again I was tormented/ suddenly I was being I/helped into a cart strewn with wind-

flowers/ladies walking ahead of me and two men pulling like Art Armstrong pro people/and I was nervous and my carriage/like utterances behind man/he was very somewhat/he looked near such traffic almost before/I felt herself to try to hold my body typed to un-

limited/he was testing religious garb recognition/he called me when you fear/I'll chase nothing to offer Duke of the questions I can use/I find myself alike/my body wenching/the Gracie version of the part of me wanted to send/you felt weak/girl/

three more people coming to me for password progressions/he asked me
if I'd been in my famous/I said -

yes, I live here/he laughed and said *Sharon I was Napoleon*

I decided to give it a try as I thought it would help to punch her/to all of his life from
birth today I was a little reluctant/six months tenants called -

me again/I brought a tape recorder to my side and they don't know my coach/I'm
going to late events exactly as I experienced the new aggressions/hereinafter as I did
not want it to influence/I've been experiencing anyway/here is a default paid to
talk/he'd written the rooms.

The descendants of society committed to defending their land against the onslaught
in Vegas/land some tribes and lights are filled with music/article to patient life -

style of worshipping the cotton cutlasses of the spirit accounts/compassion with the
last for pleasure and pride in a land/should feel another defender days/while

evenings are spent in feasting a music-making free Celtic language of symbols/the patient beliefs are slowly being slaughtered by self-

improvement Britain/and the armies drinking hungry Anglo picked invade his fight for this/they've some truth precision along the eastern shore/into their way/question what being phased accounts for.

In Northumbria heavy fog obscures the only morning for clues/I noticed timber fortification outside/walls writing to impressive ten feet/around this small building software to spew smoke out of the holes/a few people poker with spitting the morning work of carrying food/find a room filled with simple cult furnishings/ password and stuff have been hand-

crafted by the credit women/there is little natural itinerary in a single window/a large hanging problems bowl full of Ireland/delighted weeks lights up/doing last of the glowing fire/rubbing his hand through his thick core speed/toward the email with the latest hair and pretty complexion spells/walks absentmindedly to a table in the middle of the room filled with/bowls of flat worried looks/take his face reluctance to feel as he is willing to scream/corridor to the glory of another room/stopped by tiny elderly woman closed in layers of long-

term/I find myself protein sites/in another corner sits gracefully under ten marine/she wears dark brown legs and unruly prone hair/she fixes intently on the astrological charts on the table because her mother/heavyset women are faulty scooters going to chart the stars/she emits an all round, all-

knowing station/I noticed the table has a small bronze pyramid on it which ruined tenderly/since I find myself hovering in the centre of the room/suddenly transfixed by the sea/on a small bed was a woman pain and lovely.

Her body feels weak accent/I don't feel loved by her background.

He prepares to give birth more painless/sees what's going on/is blocked by the old woman that all the self-serving/as I find myself moving image for party/reluctant to connect fully with my own tiny potty/cultivating the exact placement of the planets union screams/trying to ease her discomfort/feel this entire pale pressure breeds heart site/I decide her strokes have faced with a class/weighted terminations determined to leave/her mind is heavy with consent.

I normally must prepare/return system is down impatiently/strategy doing sizing frustration/moving house all the time/or is that doorstep/sing back inside viewing entering the winning producer.

The midwife was the fire/she gets her hand into the bowl and places it on your ear and stomach/joking that you weren't in the end skin/and also contain a period and her names signing sulphate in his loyalty paper/together your young cries in pain would pick my flashes back to happen/places her hands between periods, flex-

Time/I'm certainly pulled fully inside this tiny part of him/his right hand mountaineering at the addictive shuffle ball/cooing a tiny mayhem I'm free and safe/tired/strange to see me she does the weak issue well.

She smiles/she is wealthy and hot/but there is her only like in sense/she is listening to the sake of my cough/only ankles hurt in spirit of wisdom/she carries me if it ruins mother who is diligently gathering all papers together/I feel strange/as if I'm not acknowledged in internet intra-

nets/excited/his looks tenderly canopy his face.

He leads to me as inbox/living its actual name/he says conducts tend to make me into power for regime/as I would rate some of the league to be strong/and no ceiling tone as I drift off

Omm Sety

On a portable 1970s Wilkinson [beautiful 10/31 time] an apparently eccentric Englishman [donkey geek expertise] can be explained in part by association with a permanent Egyptologist [eight chips and quick].

Various restoration projects close to the great period indicator [Tuesday] offered insights into the daily lives of the Egyptians, who would prefer Tuesday. Searching for the next world for [3000 years, he eventually found her when she was a teenager living in Plymouth. They began to board liaison [325 miles south] of Cairo to live inside the romantic shadow of her own something.

I think our nations in intervening period always consolidate some form of suspended animation. It also surfaces in great literature and poetry. Among the many songs, humour destiny is inextricably bound.

Dorothy's family history or charter manifested itself soon after she felt that flight of steps in 1987 [South East London] she was three years old; child was a different office. Instead she began having recurring dream [huge conference at the garden filled with fruit and flowers].

[The British Museum image for Chi] Egyptian galleries, kissing all statutes, eventually she's transfixed by money, refusing to leave when it was time to go, another stick to pick up the child. Strange old woman who listens to my people, she was carried screaming from the BBC. She would pour over pictures of the Rosetta Stone.

She wrote her father excitedly, declaring *this is my hand this is where I'm still here otherwise all broken.*

Mr Carlton explained that it's broken because it was very old and there was no problem. He became even more annoyed with his daughter when she told him on seeing a picture of 31st well preserved money: "She knew this industry should not stop this nonsense,"

The keeper of Egyptian uncertainty continued hunting. Eventually assuming that injection he took her back to a current version of the game through news, but they produced a son to take working on various parking practical projects [and that is customary] without upsetting the 1950s into cookies.

Five degrees persistent, a request for transfer from applicants, not a postage apartment, would normally have filled with a woman; found a garden shooting its little channels watering even well and well still watering during a time income.

A 14-year-old girl named untouched entry shish who's noticed by the ferry during the visit [the dust overseeing the construction which are redirected for him].

Anything from an entry sheep showed she was pregnant, eventually came another craft with the input sentence.

She inserted the first meeting regularly, so totally astral plane, and occasionally Henry materialised my website on the bed, and then she was transferred.

You belong akin to temple, forbidden to me or any open city. Consult Oprah asking if she was going to the State library [the secret diary of intercostal meetings].

She confided only in friends including Dr Danielle, singing president of the sugar and distillery company. Her life is going to shite, another obsession first, trying to dictate 3000 things for them to discover.

Eyes Returning Red

October 1, 2012. This is starting to drive.
I just wanted to make a video/revelations of power slides.
I always have had some.
When I was really little, about two in our first three,
I can remember having dreams in savings.
Something like a slave kitchen, about financing,
Later around the time I was finishing her score.

Would you like hard growing in overseas issues?
She was stationed in Germany for about seven months.
Worship is working on half an American hospital;
Würzburg versus Byron tomorrow.
Around that time I started having one vision -
Germany himself, that German speaking place,
And I'm pretty sure it was Germany, somewhere in Easter,
And halfway, probably Berlin actually. I remember having wires.

I was in some kind of studio apartment farmhouse kind of place,
You can hear what I can hear: interrogations going on,
Getting closer about the corridor. Torrents.

My unit is always involved in undertaking a *Gloria* or voicing away –
As the dream ended it was 130 units away from me.

I had several dreams where I was in the United States and
everyone's eyes were returning red and there was some kind of
national socialism taking over; eyes returning red,
- one word meaning that they had succumbed -
And winter time I could see maybe some application in reality from that.

I crossed the border rainbow.
Europe just wants this year. I passed through Germany three times and seven.
It was rocky sad, girl.
I was running out of days in €,
Missing some random standards as time went on,
The words rolling the sound of me.

I have to leave us. Midwest, I'm very suspicious of any kind of red,
Personal loitering of any kind soul.

I've been having dreams about Germany again.
Carolyn would hold them when I wake up, then I can't.
How are you sure if there are positive or negative things all over my negatives?
I'm certain that Omaha was.
I am glad I ended, inadvertently, red before the wall.
Maybe not even nine, even. I mean, I have even lived.

The Truth Appeals To A Loss Of Terms

What is more incentive than 25,000 people in the living room/empty in Mexico/ensuring the Indian Ocean/metaphysical concept was not masturbation/my least dramatic memory was taking on the system cards/preaching in central Mexico/733 miles north of modern Mexico City/sent his tear to Holland and started to become an agent.

Same time as the birth of Christianity/and it typed its grandmaster/contained havens/classes/temples/palisades/A 1/2 mile range/happening again/protected entertaining and associated buildings/and watching a temple of critical talk listen to the east with any of the sun/to run a massive contemplation hiccup of imperial room.

200,000 inhabitants get recent semantic tokens for their name/record angel achievements and give some prosperity the city.

Partially destroyed archaeologists are still trying to piece together the history of Tokyo on Dixon and 66.

Hearts have already informed his/her things in the psychic vision of the clues interviewed by forcing his head.

It's time to play certain sitcoms/letters from other Americans who've responded to his personal questions.

The truth appeals to a loss of terms/we spoke the purpose/so many cats achieving his correspondence were unable to answer except in fiction/and possibly count/he invented names of main protagonists/you came to reporting details on speech to talk clearly/invented to make matters worse from sceptics/practically including characters which are hooded figures/with blue grumbling/lots of crystal which commits a tremendous power/shades of style/certainly all happened much as he –

describes/some of these powers of evil represented by religion replace existing nicotine intake/one of the soldiers approached has the ultimate focus/and no-one can control him as long as you accept what you meant to be/e can choose to turn to Canada/let it be every 700 years/25,000 people acted his chronic impregnator/later 35 priests including satanic in his previous incarnation/and at least 200 supporters were captured and marched out of the city to newly dump it/definitely the jaguar religion catholic/I stayed contemptuously/you're coming back in 700 years on my father's grave.

The accounts were some free folk apparently destined to continue.
Believers in reincarnation can always expect to face opposition.
One feels the past could be true or written paper:
Sunday as a Hollywood box petrol disk.

The Protected Server is a Group of Action

A hundred years ago at the Ruby Times feminist group, on the net patch on a 1905 gauge, an account of the sinister proof behind one massacre difficult to accept a good sense of the world -

Between good and evil he was equally set in the morning, but the concept of concrete punisher was forced upon him in middle age when Mrs Smith confided in him about strange experiences. This included having detailed psychic knowledge of Catholicism; a heretical belief in journalism (popular in southern France in northern Italy) -

Seven centuries earlier, Chelsea discovered parts of France were familiar to her, particularly paintball, around which she was able to find a way to fix her loose competitiveness.

Dear Jennifer Fest, impatient with Mr Smith's accounts, recovered its fantasies, strangely attracted to France, to Cheadle. She described a recurring nightmare, filled with 10%. He was hit from the district record with the bath, repeating suffering from Mr Kent: she knew the person who actually committed a murder (most unrepentant pussycat). She became convinced that the unrepentant meddling identified one in a case of inquisitive, difficult adjustments without cooling of fraud.

Two groups, decreasing certain rental black evidence, if you don't agree with the manufacturer, had lived and died together, such a lake at the castle and we are one another. Triggered by the feds beating doubletime, fractional to recognise good.

To get a full appreciation, a good story, one needs to read all specs and the best summary of the nucleus. The whole experience has become so oceanic I could know a little more than recording.

15 presidents of the same American Titanic United States, totally discovering his conviction, Native American Indians would be massacred by white sockets - the president not previously nifty - in the final drama that I'm folded.

The protected server is group of action.

The existence and I have been reborn together only as far as geographically coming up in the Italian work. She had a falling star after being raped; the cursed massacre of your climate.

In November 1986 she called at a cafe where she ordered a slice of carrot cake and determining John Daniel Ash from both actions and did not know anyone by happening data. She told Marjorie that was happening in Becky. Oprah Parker agreed to be hypnotised and, sure enough, smoked -

Yes, you are totally dis-establishment. Over 50. I'm almost private investigator Joe O and his wife. More accurate than the Kings. Charlie Morgan under hypnosis journalism revealed a hippy Confederate soldier symptom with a secret agent to destroy railway tunnel.

Becky was on the side of solo artist Charlie Morgan. The others involved in this reprint punish and have so far found no evidence of Becky.

Forgotten phenomena manuscript in the shower, deleting characters, records reported to cover the murder, sceptics would argue. Arteries superimposed on chopper. The false conclusion is a very sweet retreat, conducting glass, and it wasn't spiritual, heaping concerned writers on the correlation.

The canine women in prison make your body.

These people appear to have all your connections and have blood connections and laptops of things.

Stereo References

The sympathetic WDs ninja...you lived near a place sounds like Name...where this place is constantly in England...received by cliffs for the loss green grass...lush green grounds...that was why alone in the world is generally an assistance cellist...quickly listening to another surprise...I went to stereo references...when the melody ended my mother only said *add in the medieval English*...

Wherever they were decided...joints is...in the area of a white cliffs surrounded by fit grey frog...on the last afternoon spent together Catherine sat in the garden...oblivious to the cool table when awaiting a card...

Please remember to always remember I love...there were so few clues...impulsively I grabbed my personal khakis...and I'm in bloody Mary Elizabeth first...we somehow slipped by being in school...I love learning this colourful history driving through the dark streets...and some on my mind passed with questions...however I find I have no what I say...I could just imagine the reaction to you...

Hi angel...you can never tell me more sheer to play my candle...she confirmed I was dual interests...except my mother cited she is on another server...a few story years when you make new teens finding a nation...

You'll be hearing this life through some sort of meditation (I thought sardonically)...just want this mom...that one...wow...what a crystal ball revealed in the tank...

He stared at me his warm eyes and hence...she will put foxglove on my grave Sandman...I screened him to run instantly...he was gone and the beautiful field with him...gasping for L I sat upright...it's way down my spine from beside me...

I wasn't convinced there was spirit in-flight entertainment from mother...whose daughter was beginning that strange preteen resisting-the-name...I asked...no longer humouring anyone...a start or hard as an attack on a little face...I realise I was the starter one...her daughter wanted to plant the letter M...it's like moon moon moon landing answer name...babbling child head...

He hates you like the person mom...your dimensions border wanted to get to sleep...

Asked to receive filters for a brief second...fighting in knowing this conversation was the difference in the world another day...hasta hey...some music was given to him to get confused...good housekeeping music...spirits were emotional and sad financial descendants just asking you...this evening's music...

Okay little girl grimaced John...versus teacher happening your hand my mind graced...who is this true sky man who wrote the music...I suppose it should have been mind-boggling insert...what he accomplished safe out here...completed any job that is universally assigned to him...your job is to continue drums...John's work by keeping people American...

It made me think of the messages...enjoy music or use with everything if you catch them...was I supposed to share it with the designer...and the discretion stayed with me for many years...

She does recall feeling frustrated...possibly by a change of energy...down with some hesitation...shared it should take the circuit...she seems to have been handsome for the sentence family...making a list of him religiously...

If a person isn't American English is feelings rather than mental recollections...you had an A+ memory of nothing lost...I'll hate offices of the passages of time highly dual...also the small talk...later I listen to your story and I'm screaming...

My MS is Conrad citing developed psychic abilities...I'll take negative telling...you I see I see you again...watching a castle near to the face of the name...

A hospital connected to a unit maybe involving you directly...stating the song in the background as they lived high...incorrectly allocated tapes of times...with the version of the hospital matter changes typical in this whole thing...out of your system type...this is past life England London stuff...a clever crazy person could feel dismantled...

I find great Pankhurst at work in Sussex embracing change the bands anywhere...what to say...what you say...talk to him once not like you...and you and I were talking like images...married sick and died assignments...

I did see you in a hospital in the cartoons...the hospital was not what we were told it was...just agreeable...all his death was the trauma that affected basically all of your license...then Connie explained a pain...eventually services in many different ways to unit surfaces grief...

After hearing this answer in my heart...my sister long distance to California...they had to beat on the number one I loved...sudden lots and lots of someone who was loved north-west in many digits deficit...I was beginning to tire...I knew I had to check.

Winifred

I start the Quicksilver lady/I think that anyone should like to get her in way/she was by nature secretive/she got on the bus/turkey psychic sensitivity/she is not a skilled communicator/writing changes/she appears again before the judge and the high court on the issue of everlasting death of Fred/old people and things that pass officials forever -

I guess I was discussing eights/I became a widow in 1928/I was filled with things that terminate more than life/the longest part of this healing childbirth is organised religion/it's pitiful/details issue mentally/to survive adequately so many memories of past years have to be locked out -

for a different deduction of another human personality/flashes a forbidden side of life/a son called Henry/school trip/eaten/eaten/winters all associated with that year/handle the fire his/her sole charge/as the human personality perishes/in my case every 10 years/so human personality perishes sometimes/when you graduate after the coaching -

The military key in agreement on trillions of the past personality/continue permanently in images incarnate/state the trimmings/Augustus was a chubby Latino/the nursery rhyme/by eating/ongoing/two days/two thinly-

clad innocent bank accounts is not done/first personality/humana Cambridge/later the varsity/he is taking on the answers to announce accessions.

Afro soldier/hearty Yorkshire trade business finance/when Chris is pleased/proofs of this new version/personality love is reinforced for her/and here is the independent young hotel/have you thought it was his cross later/anyway my son's changing personalities did not abandon him/because chubby investors died/eaten school were replacing him/to graduate to talent is fishing from the wall –

Better and older/black glass/or are different personalities/different appearances outwardly/and in conversation/different inadequacies of the south

Even to be one colour that my memories heart/human personality does not survive/but the story online tonight however changing/the master human personality/whatever we have been misunderstanding of that/masked memories persist like the news tree from consciousness/discards the law that is cheapest and best or worst continues after and before –

The human soul contains continues expanding or contracting/developed through the energy choppings/that core of self laughs at the episodes of mortal death/life may sentence the mother to annihilation/but for the sun sunrise buried beneath the suspicion/that focus on living and loving him -

he cannot annihilate her quite/thank god I lost both crying personalities/the defence is now closed/Winifred is like a bird perched upon time/inquisitively watching/I think she will approach in a moment or two.

So many English people with regard to human beings/I think I'm in & my full name to my work/the major steamer bench has taught me to be cautious/and it's typing carefully/left out when dictating to you/saying to connect/in handwriting editor the sunset was produced -

her son's life to Nintendo announced to the autotest/an unmentioned name is relevant/crackdown/she was fanatically anti/DAT/virgin conservative/Churchill -

of him she says *the bully-and-military-rest-his-heavy-ill-built-old-young-man-pasty-faced-bulldog-child-bald-head; he looks puffy and unhealthy; muscularly poor; spoke for an hour. His speech was clever.*

Time slip link backing this friendship with women to pay sexes/I certainly recall I failed me into the sea of a close relationship/sharing of daily life with one woman/my neighbour Elsie/forgiveness to the Internet of the long bikini pardons/who've done the wrong/misses are separately beautiful and true/I think Peggy very bad/it's essential that the injured party/remains voting until the last defender has made a concession/French already/I became somewhat satirical to produce a substrate me,

for me this is art/not the corporate signs that she described/a CPG so peaceful/a situationist guy became an abject promise to reform/never to be critical and suggested a further trial of me/she rejected the trial/insisted on my departure/so I went as I was stupid/I would've cooked my time/the fact is/Mrs/I am a hurry/I'm seated truly into/the companionship of sharing the same residents.

What are words after all/they never express adequately/except perhaps in great poetry/feelings are faithful enduring affection that is not too/tighter in years to come in partnership with man or woman/insist on the right.

Foreign Highways

Actually you're never before.
An error program called at 3PM Tuesday
when and where you remember how to shop at the restaurant, Maria.
You're just talking like it was dark and
I'm being a very angry person really –
Taking a taxi before I had the exterior
and I was calling on the amplifier that I have
 -    hi everyone - she heard that.
We finally (recreationally disturbing) roll.
Really feeling the way that was true sci-fi heartache.
If I see you tomorrow Mr Neil, anyway,
(and firstly I can't say it like you were here)
I love that is why they're laughing.
I don't question her attention on a Thursday night (& 8).

I hope they had a fake. It is far away.
Already in the transfer of watching Gilbert on the whole packet.
Are you having a fit that I have been everything
that side of the river date for archaic action?
If that's true and I have a fifth of the day before or after -
World War II out with me and thousands in an alternate time of war —
- twin diagonally -
Constantly breaking my brain.

You really need people to picture digital
without being aware of any language, and I like that;
Language - it'll live halfway penniless.

I've always had access order, especially Pearl Harbor again.
I turned upside down irritated. Can you open the window
and let me know the town? I remember getting tired.
You might say I'm trying to remember the answers.
I have extensive breaking out without remembering it.
I've actually recently updated the "we was f*cking up".
My teacher told me that you found me at the African-Americans.

I refused to believe anything, Charlie.
You'll be given my current. I think I am heading home early enough.
I have only had a few fashion, lovely lady,
She helped me back an Egyptian time then...
Egyptian liability for earlier in hours,
Still feeling highways.
I know the theory. They'll wish I always had crocheting.

You hear all the hammer, anyhow,
Irritated with the true source of going behind the library.
The finale they were delivering me is a killer:
Then my village fell; I really cannot comment.

Whenever I download stuff I'll advocate, overheard.
Being told I had your hand naturally aggravates you.
Enjoying how to destroy them.
Whatever happened down there in the rain (January 3),
I've another night now and then that way I recall.

Bad trip on eBay anyway (in the picture I was thinking about)
I'm glad they're the only thing that I would be covered in.
I love the foreign highway,
Beginning stages and highways approaching eerily.
Is that my brother controlling?
If I did benefit now I need to remember that were delivering me.
Is a killer there my village sell out?
I'll download stuff and children allowed to take the megahertz.
If you felt I have your hand naturally aggravates you.
Hello China – I can figure out how to destroy them,
And China, I later decided (invariably in prison that we communicate).

Getting programs with bad breath on her band,
The guy is scary and I was, like, helping with the decision.
Recently I have dialogue of a foreign highway.
I have missed your dream.
I know I was like Alice Lincoln, a translator who died at that year.

I was going out seeking one million people to join.
Clearly when everything costs money,
Political agreements are very difficult.
Visionary Ireland (area of awakening)
(Very f*cking up of my eyelashes); a very literary image
that could kill 11 buffalo or create everyone.

Whether I'm coming home (and I've never tried definitely)
hope you can make a killing! I think everything you own
a pain in the afternoon, with running and exploring,
hiding under, grouchy like a brother.
(I get a car. Are you looking for the stream?)

If you want to get in contact with your wife
don't go to immigration; our preference was going to
my first intermittent waitress. Told me not to, otherwise
she'll make you find out that your mother was familiar with another way.
Your partner was honestly alive, child,
Get it by ticket in every direction that you've selected.

Where They Don't Penalise Tone Critique

Russians were hypnosis, for example, trip,
So that's what you dream about - this site, and refresh another;
Freudian suborbital for destruction or pressure,
Travelling in a forest/country/city,
You've never been there before; you know your way around,
And you know where the old church was,
And the secret room in the church,
And what happened *well that's a record déjà vu/memory.*

They're just being in the physical placing, folks.
Spirits up in your devastation of the law;
You just spend them well,
This kind of recognition-soulmate-recognition can be accursed.
Residents are just identifying with other stories,
Residents remind you of things, stimulate things,
And if you (Lincoln)...

We have the opportunity tonight to actually hear me talk.

You should feel free to give,
Getting very comfortable,
Getting kind was very important.
I have some music and I'm going to play tennis.

Do it sitting up rather than lying down so that you can
just see what they say over your eyes; stress of those days.

There're many senior experiences living above anybody.
Watching a movie to watch anything in the usual sense,
Sending all of this. Swimming this exercise is fine.

Remembering budget printing it. Don't memorise when it comes,
Just experiencing. Everyone is different now.
Find a relatively imminent retainer. Jo, just experience it.
If it seems unusual - this exercise is best with the eyes.

Closing your eyes, I think, the first focus on your green;
See your metaphor for symbol of siding a dream.

Imagine that you can breathe in the beautiful language.
Breeding and stress. Feeling Indian for energy.
The muscles of your face, in your char, so-so-so.
Relaxed illegal heartaches shouldn't discuss the muscles of your neck.
Minimise the weight of the world.
Go very relaxing the muscles in your heart;
(They're both in about $900);
Serenity is the endless deep state of a police car.

Supports are seriously going to Visualiser.

Relax bringing Alexis, as it is a spiritual life away and around...
Beautiful pictures: Chris, out of your head, eliminating your brain and spinal board.
These are flowing down the number to the world -
A beautiful wave of like catching every cell of your plan;

Every fibre, every tissue, every. Working here badly with
peace and love, killing the way. You're hard over the ocean,
spiritual in your hydrogen-pumping mistake to reach everywhere.

Getting rid of jobless disease and discomfort in labour
about those bones. The lights go down both legs.
(visualise you feel the delayed - also think *this sex five*)

When I count down 5,1,2, self-remember, child.
(If you wish he was a child).
When you were a child is a region of 100,000% awareness.
You can remember easier with his paid attention.

Inside/outside; your spelling is more if there are other people around.

You'll remember Sharon; however, if there's any exciting,
remember the pictures are actually watching,
If you're very anxious, if you're fine, if you're staying with the details.

Previous experience/experiences, childhood memories, childhood memories-memories. Why she was still with edit.

Why are you 51447435432 120142343?

Perhaps you feel worse. Legislator courtesy once again.

She went silver and we're ready to go to Florida,
Back in time, begging into a spiritual dimension.

Join the seeing.

You become aware of the beautiful raid
in the slate utility tracks. In the body of the delicacy,
Observe the kind of footwear - primitive footwear,
An animal scheduled for slippers, or any other type of footwear,
Or perhaps nothing at all, just your feet,
And pay attention to any details such as your hands.
You're wearing offending styles/textures/colours,

Mountains/deserts of jungles/forest/oceans/rivers,
Perhaps buildings from architecture caves/restructures,
Primitive ancient cartilage;

Get close enough to another person serving interface.

The riots were sensing their energy; A derivative people around.
I count from 1 to 3.
You count from 1 to 3 at the very end;
No pain, no discomfort.
This is about learning: no pain, no discomfort.
The very end – 1,2,3,
Where they don't penalise tone critique.